Advanced Praise

"'P is for Palestine' *is a colorful manifestation of all that is beautiful about the land of my parents and ancestors. This book is a gift that takes you on a journey of love, life and resilience; the virtues of my beloved Palestine.*"
—**Linda Sarsour**, award-winning Palestinian Muslim American activist.

"*You will fall in love with this innovative, much needed, and beautifully illustrated Palestinian alphabet book. Highly recommended!*"
—**Dr. Jack G. Shaheen**, author of "Reel Bad Arabs: How Hollywood Vilifies a People" and a foremost authority on media images of Arabs and Muslims in American Popular Culture.

"*This book provides an attractive and thoughtful introduction to the heritage and culture of Palestine that will be appreciated by children whose families come from Palestine, and by children everywhere.*"
—**Dr. Rashid Khalidi**, globally renowned Palestinian-American scholar, author, and the Edward Said Professor of Modern Arab Studies at Columbia University.

"*This powerful book will prove to be pivotal for so many young Palestinians on their search for identity and belonging, and will introduce countless others to a place and people that have been marginalized for too long in their struggle for equality. I can't wait to buy copies for my niece, and her friends. P is for 'Palestine', and also for 'Proud.'*"
—**Ahmed Shihab-Eldin**, Palestinian-American Emmy-nominated journalist, broadcaster, and senior correspondent for AJ+.

"*G for GREAT . . .*
P for PEACE IN PALESTINE."
—**Marwan Bishara**, internationally renowned Palestinian author, broadcaster and chief political analyst at Al Jazeera Media Network and host of its flagship show EMPIRE.

"Golbarg Bashi's 'P is for Palestine' is a moving journey of alphabetical letters becoming a bridge, a boat that connects us to our homeland and our heritage, while yearning for freedom & peace in Palestine."
—**Rula Jebreal**, award-winning Palestinian author, film-maker (*Miral*), journalist, and foreign policy analyst.

"I wish I had a book like this when I was a child! Fantastic and fun . . . a great way to show children another world and open their minds. It's especially exciting to me as a Palestinian as I always want to find ways to show my baby she can feel proud of her culture and have fun at the same time. Colorful, truly original and a delight for young and old!"
—**Annemarie Jacir**, Academy Award nominated Palestinian Filmmaker (*When I Saw You*).

"I'm so happy to live in a world where a book like **'P is for Palestine'** exists. If I had had something like this as a child, I would have felt so much less alone and so much more interested in my culture, instead of wondering why no one else seemed to know the words that were so comforting and real to me. I cannot wait to give a copy to my niece, nephew, and every other little Arab American child, who will not only be able to learn from this book, but will also be able to feel proud of where she is from, and, consequently, rooted deeply in the world."
—**Najla Said**, Palestinian-American playwright, actress and author of "Looking for Palestine: Growing Up Confused in an Arab-American Family."

"A book for our children that teaches self-love and pride. A book for our friends that shares a central piece of our lives. A book for ourselves that sings without apology: **'P is for Palestine'** and all of its wonders that make it home."
—**Noura Erakat**, internationally renowned Palestinian-American human rights attorney, academic and activist.

"Golbarg Bashi takes children (and parents) into Palestine, illustrated beautifully with Golrokh Nafisi's drawings. **'P is for Palestine'** is a must for anyone who grew up with fragmented past and is looking to changing today's stereotypes."
—**Najwa Najjar**, award-winning Palestinian filmmaker (*Eyes of a Thief - Pomegranates and Myrrh*).

"Palestine is our story, and our story begins with the alphabet.
Every letter a direction. Stunningly illustrated.
A dream-book for all ages."
—**Nathalie Handal**, award-winning Palestinian poet and writer.

To my children Chelgis and Golchin . . .
and to all their Palestinian sisters and brothers. . .

Golbarg Bashi

***

Write down!
I am an Arab
And my identity card number is fifty thousand:
I have eight children—
And the ninth will come after a summer . . .

Mahmoud Darwish, "Identity Card" (1964)

P is for Palestine: A Palestine Alphabet Book
Author: Golbarg Bashi
Illustrator: Golrokh Nafisi
Layout: KB Studio
Copyright © 2017, Golbarg Bashi
All rights reserved under International and American Copyright Conventions.
Published in the United States by Dr. Bashi™, New York, NY.
www.drbashi.com/books
ISBN-10: 0-9990020-1-5 | ISBN-13: 978-0-9990020-1-8
Library of Congress Control Number: 2017916263
Second Edition in Dr. Bashi™ Diverse Children's Books Series, 2017
Printed in the United States of America
www.drbashi.com

P IS FOR PALESTINE

A PALESTINE ALPHABET BOOK

by

GOLBARG BASHI

Illustrated by

GOLROKH NAFISI

Can we sing the ABC anywhere?
With a woolly bear or on thin air?

Yes! Let's align.
We're going on an alphabetic adventure to
P A L E S T I N E !

3

4

A is for **Arabic**, my tongue, a language that's the 4th biggest ever sung!

B is for **Bethlehem**, my birthplace with the best Baklawas, put it on a plate not in a vase!

C is for **Christmas**, coziest in Jesus Christ's country, with the crunchiest candy!

D is for **Dabkeh,** a delightful dance. Daddy's done it even in Sundance!

E is for **Eid**, it means Festival, like the Muslim *Eid al-Fitr* when we eat enticing eats, get excited over gifts, and enjoy seeing our extended families!

F is for **Falafel**, fresh, fast food, everyday's good fuel!

G is for **Gaza**, a city like Mombasa without any plazas, but full of generous casas!

H is for **Handala**, hear his hellos, he is our hero!

I is for **Intifada**, Intifada is Arabic for rising up
for what is right, if you are a kid or a grownup!

J is for **Jesus**, Jesus was born in my hometown (Bethlehem), not in Jamestown!

K is for **Kuffiya**, the best kind you can hang on a hook in Hebron souk!

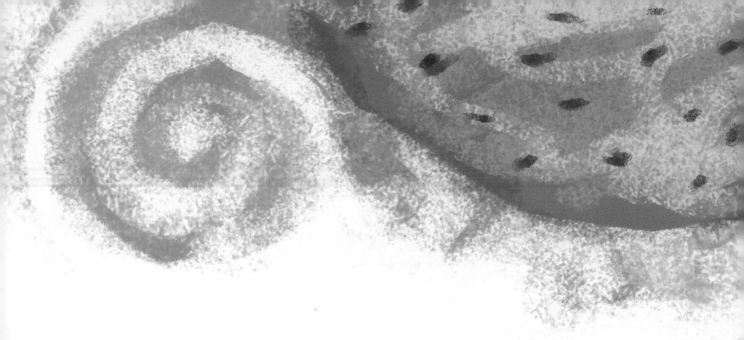

L is for **Labneh**, Labneh is like yogurt. I eat it for lunch, wearing my loafer!

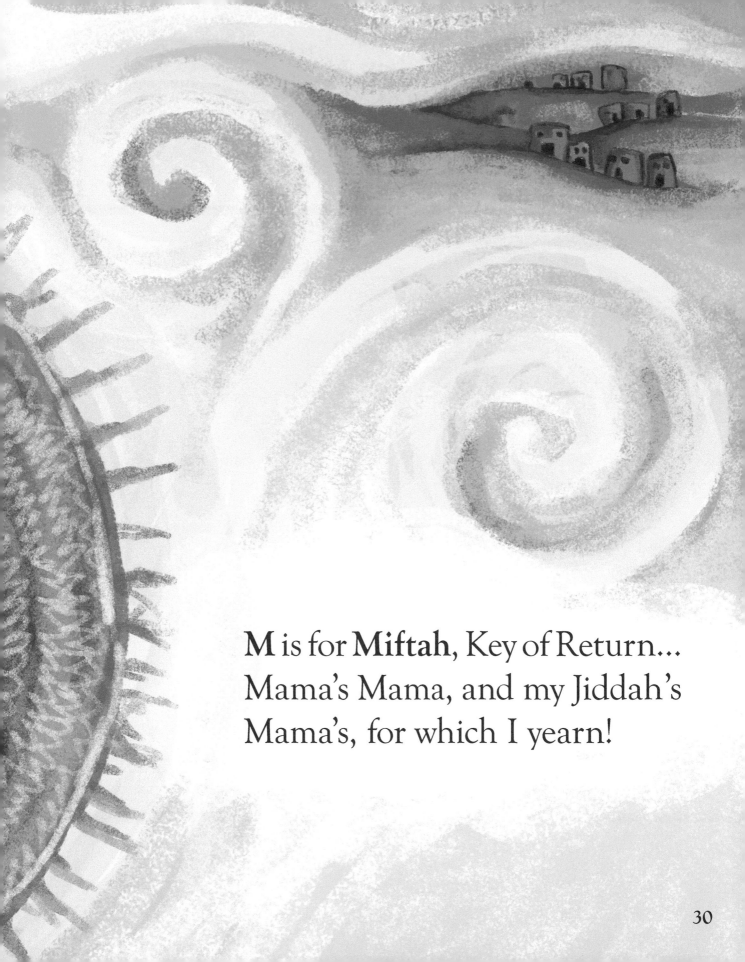

M is for **Miftah**, Key of Return...
Mama's Mama, and my Jiddah's
Mama's, for which I yearn!

N is for **Nazareth**, or En-Nasra in Arabic.
Nestled in the North with narrow lanes...
Sundays are its noisiest days!

O is for **Olives** and **Orange Orchards**, yummy fruits of our land, good for me, for you and all of our friends!

P is for **Palestine**, Precious to me and my people, evergreen like a forest pine!

Q is for **Quds,** home to the picturesque Qubbat As-Sakhrah (Dome of the Rock) where we quietly go for our daily barakah.

R is for **Ramallah,** where rainbows come after the rain, inshA'llah!

S is for **Souk**, a market where
Shatwehs shimmer and sparkle!

T is for **Thob**, a traditional dress with tatreez (embroidered pieces). Takes time to make, with thousands of tiny threads, if you please!

U is for **'Um & 'Ukht**, 'Umi is my mother, 'Ukhti's my sister. Our language is Arabic but we speak English too! How about You?

V is for **Vine**, my favorites are grape vines, David picks them and makes Waraqa Dawali, oh so divine!

W is for **Wallahi**, "I swear by God," my writing teacher says that her name is Wodd, isn't that odd?

X is for **Xylophone**, exercise playing it for Dabkeh just as you'd do on a saxophone!

Y is for **Yallah!** Stop yawning, come see the village of Yubla...

Z is for **Za'atar**, full of zest and a must have in our kitchen's chest!

Appendix

Arabic is the official language of the Palestinian people. Arabic is the official language of 25 countries and some 300 million people speak it as their mother tongue spread across West Asia and North Africa. It is used by approx. 1.3 billion Muslims around the world in their daily prayers and to read their holy book The Qur'an in its original classical Arabic (as revealed to the Prophet Mohammed in 610-632).

Bethlehem is the birthplace of Jesus Christ, a Palestinian city located in the central West Bank, Palestine, about 10 km (6.2 miles) south of Jerusalem. Its population is approximately 25,000 people.

Casa means home in Spanish. The proverbial phrase "mi casa su casa" ("my home is your home") has become a universal expression of kindness and hospitality.

Christmas is the Christian festival celebrating the birth of Jesus Christ, as described in the holy Bible. It is a big event in Christ's Palestinian homeland.

Dabkeh is a traditional Palestinian group dance also practiced in Lebanon, Syria and parts of Iraq. It is performed in weddings, festivals.

Eid means Festival in Arabic. It lends its name to Christian, Jewish, Muslim or any other religious holiday, e.g. Christmas is *Eid-e Milad*, the Jewish Passover celebration in Spring is named *Eid al-Fasah*, and the Muslim festival celebrating the end of Ramadan (month of fasting) is named *Eid al-Fitr*.

Falafel is a deep-fried ball made from ground chickpeas or fava beans. Falafel is a widely popular food, commonly served inside the pocket of a flatbread known as "pita."

Gaza is a Palestinian territory on the eastern coast of the Mediterranean Sea bordering Egypt.

Handala is the name of a cartoon character illustrated by the late Palestinian political cartoonist Naji Al-Ali (1938-1987). Handala is always seen bearing witness to injustices, his back turned to readers. He is the symbol of the Palestinian resistance.

Intifada means "uprising" in Arabic, marking specifically the struggle of Palestinians to gain freedom and independence.

Kuffiya is a widely popular Arab headdress created from a square scarf, usually made of cotton.

Labneh is a thick creamy type of yogurt eaten in Palestine and other Mediterranean nations.

Miftah means key in Arabic. It is a symbol of the Palestinian right of return to homes left behind.

Nazareth (En-Nasra in Arabic) is the name of a large city in northern Palestine. It is the historical childhood hometown of Jesus Christ with many monasteries and churches as well as Muslim holy shrines.

Quds is the Arabic name for Jerusalem, a city located on a plateau between the Mediterranean and the Dead Sea.

Qubbat As-Sakhrah is the Arabic name for Dome of the Rock, an Islamic holy site in the Old City of Jerusalem.

Ramallah is a Palestinian city in the central West Bank located 10 km (6 miles) north of Jerusalem.

Souk is the Arabic name for a marketplace or Bazaar.

Shatweh is the Arabic name for a tapered hat worn by married women in the Bethlehem area.

Thob is the Arabic name for popular Palestinian dress for women and girls. It is often decorated with embroideries, the geometric style and color signifying where it is made.

Tatreez is Arabic for cross-stitching embroideries.

'Um is Arabic for mother. Before last-names became the norm, Arab women would be known as 'Um (Mother of) followed by the name of their firstborn.

'Ukht is Arabic for sister.

Waraqa Dawali is a Palestinian dish made of grape vines stuffed with vegetables, rice and minced beef.

Wallahi is an informal Arabic word meaning "I swear by God" or simply "Believe me," "True story" or "You've got to hear this one."

Yallah is an Arabic word meaning "Let's get to work."

Yubla is a small de-populated village in northern Palestine.

Za'atar is a zesty Palestinian herb, used like oregano on freshly baked bread.

Publisher's Note

The story of Palestine is the story of our humanity. It is the story of all people, all nations, throughout history, seeking a pride of place. Anyone who has ever been to Palestine (to some also known as the Holy Land) or who has Palestinian friends, colleagues, or neighbors knows that this proud nation, located on the western-most point of Asia, not that many nautical miles away from Cyprus, Alexandria (Egypt) and Greece, is at the center of our world. It is home to the sweetest oranges, most intricate embroideries, great dance moves (Dabkeh), fertile olive groves, and sunniest people!

Inspired by Palestinian people's own rich history in the literary and visual arts, specifically by children's authors and illustrators such as Naji al-Ali (1938 - 1987), Ghassan Kanafani (1936 - 1972), and Mohieddin El Labbad (1940 - 2010) among others, an academic and children's author and a socially conscious illustrator have teamed up to create this book you are now holding—a book for children of all ages where the story of Palestine is told as simply as the English ABC...in an educational, colorful, empowering way, showcasing the beauty and strength of Palestinian culture.

We were able to publish *P is for Palestine: A Palestine Alphabet Book* by financing its publication through the crowd-fundraising platform *LaunchGood.com* and the immense support and encouragement we received from their staff Ms. Amany Killawi and Ms. Farzana Gardee. We are grateful to them and to every single person, bookstore, and institution that took a chance with our newly established publishing house and pre-purchased this book and thus made its publication a reality. We hope you are pleased with the investment you made in our vision.

To donate to Dr. Bashi™ fund for the publication of diverse children's books like *P is for Palestine*, please visit:

https://venmo.com/drbashi

www.drbashi.com